An Introduction to Courtly Jewellery

Cover and frontispiece: The Canning jewel, gold, enamelled,
set with diamonds and rubies, Italian or South German,
c. 1560: h. 10.1 cms w. 7 cms (4″ × 2¾″). M.2697–1931

An Introduction to

Courtly Jewellery

Anna Somers Cocks

Assistant Keeper, Department of Metalwork
Victoria & Albert Museum

Stemmer House
PUBLISHERS, INC.
Owings Mills, Maryland

Copyright © Anna Somers Cocks 1980
First published in 1980
by The Compton Press Ltd.
and Pitman House Ltd.
Second Impression 1982, published by
Her Majesty's Stationery Office

First published in the USA in 1982 by Stemmer House Publishers Inc.,
2627 Caves Road, Owings Mills, Maryland 21117 USA

Designed by Humphrey Stone and edited by Anthony Burton

Produced by Pitman Books Ltd, London

ISBN 0-88045-001-0

Jewellery has been worn at all times for personal adornment. Even the poor can usually contrive to wear some sort of bright knick-knack. Jewellery made of gemstones and precious metals represents wealth as well as adornment, and during the three centuries surveyed in this book, jewellery was exchanged among the rich as part of the ceremony of courtly life. Many of the pieces illustrated here are elaborate and expensive courtly jewellery, but stylistic changes can also be studied on more modest pieces.

A convenient starting point for the history of English jewellery is a sumptuary law (i.e. a law to regulate what private citizens spent on luxury goods) passed in 1363, when Edward III was King of England. This law is most revealing to anyone interested in social history and the history of jewellery. It seems that too many of the wrong sorts of people had started to wear jewellery, so that the visible differences of rank were being obscured and the wealth of the realm was being squandered. Consequently, the new law forbade handycraftsmen and yeomen to wear 'belts, collars, clasps, rings, garters, brooches, ribbons, chains, bands or seals, or any other thing whatsoever of gold or silver'; and this restriction included their wives and children as well.

This law not only provides a list of almost every sort of jewellery worn at the time, but it is a reminder that jewellery was much more than an optional personal adornment – it was also a sign of the wearer's place in society: it was part of the closely regulated ceremonial of life. Elaborate gifts of brooches, necklaces and rings were exchanged at New Year by members of the court and the princely house, and every diplomatic encounter also involved exchanges of goldsmiths' work and jewellery. For example, the accounts of the Duke of Burgundy for 1396–7 show a payment to three Italian merchants from Genoa, Florence and Lucca for jewels, among which was one that can certainly be called courtly: a gold hind with the device of the King of England, decorated with stones, which 'our Lord gave at St Omer to the Earl of Derby, when the King, our liege, and the Queen of England dined with him'.

The sumptuary law just quoted also suggests that by the mid-fourteenth century much more jewellery was being made and worn than in the previous centuries. This conclusion is perhaps supported by the fact that more pieces survive from this time than from previous periods, and is confirmed by the prominent appearance of jewellery in contemporary portraits. This latter development reaches its extreme by the second half of the 16th century, when we come upon the image of Queen Elizabeth, stiff and encrusted apparently wearing the greater part of her treasury.

Throughout the 15th and in the early part of the 16th centuries it was very common for a prince to reward faithful service with the present of a gold chain, which was easily convertible to cash. Worn around the neck or over the shoulders (PLATE 1) it was the most common sort of jewellery (apart from rings) for both men and women and many of the portraits of Lucas Cranach the Younger,

PLATE 1
Collar of SS, silver-gilt, English, late-15th or early-16th century. Croft Lyons Bequest.
41.3 cms (16¼″). M.1022–1926

PLATE 2
Rosary, Enamelled gold, English late-15th century: purchased under the bequest of Captain H. B. Murray. M.30–1934

7

PLATE 3
Left – Ring, gold, engraved with
the Trinity and two unidentified
saints, inscription inside 'en bon
an', therefore a New Year's gift,
English, late-15th century: given
by Dame Joan Evans, diam. 2.1
cms ($\frac{13}{16}$"). M. 241-1962
Centre – Seal ring, gold, set with
a medieval sapphire intaglio,
Italian, *c.* 1400: diam. 2.9 cms
($\frac{18}{16}$"). 89–1899
Right – Ring, gold set with a
diamond and ruby, the shoulders
formerly enamelled, German,
late-15th century: given by
Dame Joan Evans, diam. 2.1
cms ($\frac{13}{16}$"). M. 1-1959

PLATE 4
Crucifixion pendant, silver-gilt,
German, second half of the 15th
century: h. 6.5 cms w. 3.5 cms
($2\frac{9}{16}$" × $1\frac{3}{8}$"). 621-1906

for example, bear this out. Chains could also be a sign of allegiance to a brotherhood, political faction, or a symbol of office. The collar made of units based on the letter S, of which examples are frequently encountered in England, was in origin a Lancastrian badge but then became a sign of officialdom. Every Elizabethan judge may have worn it, and possibly also every knight. It was made in gold, silver and silver-gilt. Some such collars were gifts from the sovereign, for the household accounts show that in 1587 two gold chains of SS combined with Tudor roses were delivered to Queen Elizabeth for distribution at New Year. The SS collar survives to the present day as part of the insignia of the Lord Chief Justice of England.

In the 15th century, heraldry often provided ornamental forms for jewellery, and there were two other important types of decorative imagery, religious and amorous. Devotional jewellery was often of great richness, a fact that was not regarded as incongruous. Rosaries (sets of beads used as an aid to the recitation of prayers) were made, we know, in crystal, coral, amber, and jet. A great rarity is the late-15th century enamelled gold rosary (PLATE 2), which was found in a chest in Houghton Hall, the home of an old Yorkshire Catholic family. Each side of each bead shows a different saint, and the larger diamond-shaped units show scenes from the life of Christ. A piece which has similar religious imagery for its decoration is a gold ring·engraved with the Trinity in the centre of the bezel, flanked by two unidentified saints (PLATE 3 *left*). Quite a large number of such rings, with saints engraved on the concavities of the bezel survive and they seem to have been an exclusively English fashion.

A form of jewellery not listed in the sumptuary law, and which only evolved in the 15th century, is the pendant. Among the copious letters surviving between members of the Paston family of Norwich is one from Margaret, wife of John Paston, written in 1455, in which she asks her husband for 'sommethynge for my nekke': for when Margaret of Anjou had come to Norwich, Margaret Paston had to borrow her cousin's 'device' and she was ashamed to go among the gentlewomen in her old beads again. Many pendants were religious, like the silver gilt crucifix (PLATE 4) or the small pictorial diptych, sculpted and painted like a miniature altarpiece (PLATE 5).

The cult of courtly love, on the other hand, was the inspiration for heart-shaped brooch (PLATE 6) and for countless posy (poesy) rings. The brooch is a variation of a much older form of jewellery, the ring brooch, which had its origins in the very early middle ages, was developed in various ways in the 14th and 15th centuries, and survived in Scotland well into the 18th century. On this brooch the

PLATE 7

Left – Ring, gold, set with a table-cut jacinth, and enamelled, Italian, *c.* 1550: diam. 2.9 cms (1⅛″). 948–1871

Centre – Seal ring, gold, engraved AF, English (?), 16th century: given by Dame Joan Evans, diam. 2.7 cms (1 1/16 ″). M.228–1975

Right – Fede ring, gold and enamelled, set with a pointed diamond, German, late-16th century: given by Dame Joan Evans, diam. 2.3 cms (⅞″) M.224–1975

engraved flowers would once have held enamel. Like many posy rings, it is engraved with a loving message: 'nostre et tout ditz a votre plesir'.

It seems likely that posy rings served instead of wedding rings, which, in the form we now know, did not appear until the 18th century, and 'Fede' (i.e. faith) rings are definitely associated with marriage. They are formed sometimes as two hands holding a heart, or as two clasped hands, and they are found in silver, silver-gilt, gold, and even carved out of semi-precious stones. A very elaborate one from the late 16th century is shown on the right hand side of PLATE 7. This is also a puzzle ring and bears as an inscription on the inner sides: 'WAS.GOTT ZUSAMEN FUGET..SOLL/KEIN.MENSCH SCHEIDEN/STEIDT.IN.GOTTES.HENDEN'. (What God has joined together let no man put asunder. Stay in God's hands.)

The stylistic vocabulary of 15th century jewellery is the same as that to be found in the architecture of the period: Gothic with a flowering of naturalism – except in Italy, where Renaissance forms were appearing. Quite often, as with the pendent crucifix and diptych, jewellery was clearly a version in miniature of other forms of art – in these cases, sculpture and painting. The tracery which can be seen in church windows, on tombs and on choir stalls appears in the engraving of the silver-gilt belt buckle (PLATE 8). The rusticated cross (PLATE 9a) with its entwined branches of matted and chased gold is particularly characteristic of German late-15th century ornament –

parallels will be found in some of Dürer's designs for goldsmiths' work at this time.

The cross, in common with most of the jewellery of the three centuries covered by this book, is treated as decoratively on the back (PLATE 9b) as on the front; and, besides being set with fine stones, the whole is bright with enamelling.

The use of enamelling on the very great majority of pieces is characteristic of these centuries. In the 1400s *champlevé* and *basse-taille* continued in use from the previous centuries; a new development was *émail en ronde bosse*, a technique developed by French and Burgundian goldsmiths in the late-14th century. This meant that jewellery could be almost as multicoloured as painted sculpture. The Virgin and Child, which illustrates this point (PLATE 10) is a rare survival from around 1400 and was once part of a larger piece of jewellery such as a *morse*. Stones were, however, beginning to add greatly to the brilliance of jewellery: PLATE 3 *right* shows a late-15th century German decorative ring set with two stones which have had very different treatment by the lapidary. The diamond has been given quite a complicated 'hog-back' cut, while the ruby has merely been polished with all its natural irregularities preserved, and the two present an interesting contrast between new and old techniques.

It is now known that by the end of the 14th century Parisian lapidaries could do much more than merely table-cut the natural diamond and polish coloured stones: a diamond with as many as six facets appears in the jewellery worn by the Madonna in Jan van Eyck's Ghent altarpiece, completed in 1432, and as the fire and brilliance of the stones was released, they came to occupy a larger part in the overall design of jewels.

Another more specialised aspect of the lapidary's craft was also flourishing at this period, at least in the French and Burgundian territories, and in Italy; that is, the art of cutting *intaglios* and *cameos* on precious and semi-precious stones. One gold seal-ring (PLATE 3 *centre*) with the inscription in *Lombardic* lettering 'TECTA: LEGE: LECTA: TEGE' (read what is concealed; conceal what is read), is set with a sapphire intaglio of a woman's head which is unmistakably contemporary with the rings, and not a classical gem re-used. Both ring and intaglio are Italian and date from around 1400 and were found in 1824 at the bottom of a well in Hereford. For the whole period covered by this book seal-rings are by far the most common form of jewellery to survive, since they were an essential means of identification, and were worn by more than just the upper classes. A ring like the one just discussed must have belonged to a very rich man, but many seal-rings were quite humble, of silver or base metal, and, in the case of non-armigerous owners, often engraved with a so-called 'merchant's mark', an abstract symbol of a geometric nature. In the 16th and 17th century rings engraved with initials, often linked by a knot (PLATE 7 *centre*) became popular.

THE RENAISSANCE AND 16TH CENTURY JEWELLERY

In the course of the fifteenth century, the art of cutting cameos and intaglios flourished because of an important change which was taking place in European culture – the revival of interest in the literature and art of ancient Greece and Rome. This movement had its origin among the scholars and literati of late-14th century Italy and spread from there all over Europe, with the result that it had affected the decorative arts even of England by the 1530s.

The vocabulary of ornament changed from the naturalism, the architectural elements, and the *black-letter* inscriptions of late Gothic, to the acanthus leaf in all its forms, to cupids, grotesques, gods and goddesses, *Roman lettering*, and all the elements of classical architecture. PLATE 11 illustrates this very well. It is a hat badge, of the kind worn by men during the first half of the 16th century. It is probably English, since a number of others resembling it closely in type have English inscriptions, and it represents a Roman warrior gazing out from a roundel, such as might be found on a Roman triumphal arch, or in the Renaissance decorations carried out by Italian craftsmen at Hampton Court, which was then being built.

Another change which took place in jewellery in the course of the 16th century was that the settings of stones became more prominent. A setting had previously been a deep cup of metal surrounding the stone, with a small lobe pressed down on each side (see, for example, the settings on the cross in PLATE 9a and the ring in PLATE 3 *right*). In the next century, however, the lobes became much more prominent, and were often decorated with enamel, especially on rings (see PLATE 7 *left*).

Polychrome enamel effects, with a great deal of enamelling in the round, as on the Canning jewel (see frontispiece) were carried further and further. Of course, there was continuity with the previous century; much of the jewellery was still religious, and one of the commoner devotional pendants during the entire period was that formed as the monogram of the name Jesus, IHS, closely set with gemstones, usually diamonds. Henry VIII had one which was hung with pearls; PLATE 12 *right*, which dates from about 1560, still uses black-letter, and PLATE 12 *left* is an elaboration on this theme with three nails, symbols of the Passion, hanging from it. This, of course, is in Roman letters. Rarer, but quite common in early-17th century Spain, where there was a fervent movement devoted to the Virgin, are pendants with MARIA in monogram (PLATE 39 *right*.)

The most notable feature about the 16th century from our point of view is that more jewellery was worn than before or since, and that for the first time an appreciable quantity of it survives. In 1565, Duke Albrecht V of Bavaria founded the treasury in his palace by declaring twenty-seven pieces to be inalienable heirlooms of his princely house; in other words, his treasury could not be raided as a source of ready cash every time there was a financial crisis. Here, for the first time, is an indication that craftsmanship was beginning to be valued in addition to the intrinsic worth of the materials. Admittedly, in this case, the Duke's rule was broken, but not until the 18th century, and nine of these heirlooms have survived to the

PLATE 11
Hat badge, gold, English,
c. 1530–40: diam. 4.7 cms (1⅞″).
630–1884

PLATE 12
Left – IHS pendant, gold,
decorated with enamel and
set with diamonds, South German,
late 16th century: h. 3.5 cms
w. 5.8 cms (1½″ x 2¼″).
M.248–1923
Right – IHS pendant, gold, set
with diamonds, South German,
c. 1560: given by Dame Joan
Evans h. 3.8 cms w. 2.6 cms
(1⁷⁄₁₆″ × 1″). M.76–1975

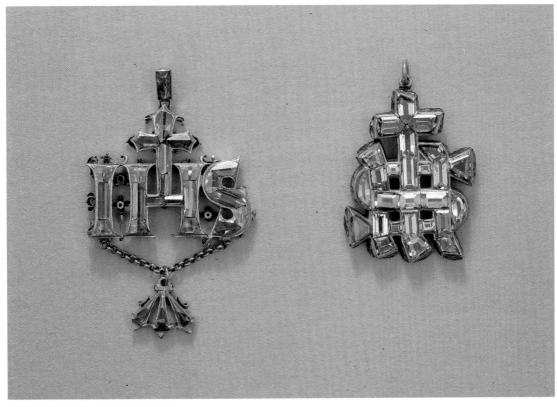

present day. Other princes copied his example, thereby ensuring that their treasuries have also come down to us, at least partially intact.

The new admiration for craftsmanship was reflected in the high esteem accorded to skilled goldsmiths, whom the various rulers of Europe cultivated, and, indeed, poached from one another. In 1573, Jacques Bylivelt of Delft was taken into service by the Grand Duke Ferdinand I de Medici, given lodgings in his Galleria in Florence, and even consulted on matters of state. A goldsmith of this sort was also involved in making bejewelled works of art such as sculptural, grotesque mounts on the semi-precious stone vessels which formed such an important part of the Mannerist treasuries, or the sparkling statuette of St George and the dragon in the Treasury in Munich.

It is also important to remember that this was the first century during which printed designs appeared in any great quantity. The craftsmen travelled but designs travelled faster, and spread ideas far beyond their country of origin. This makes it very difficult to attribute with any certainty much of the court jewellery from the different European centres. A case in point is the fashion for 'moresque' or 'arabesque', that is, an abstract, scrolling design incorporating pointed leaf shapes, which originated in the Middle East, was imported into Italy via Venice, and was adopted by numerous designers. One of these was Virgil Solis, the Nürnberg artist (1514–1562). Arabesque, introduced to England not later than 1548 when Thomas Geminus (died 1563) published his book of *Moryssce and Damashin* (FIGURE a), was widely used by English goldsmiths; for instance on the charmingly unfrightening memento mori pendant (PLATE 13) of the mid-16th century. It bears an inscription around the sides which says 'Through the Resurrection of Christe we be all sanctified', and it is known as the Tor Abbey jewel from the place

FIGURE a
An engraving from Thomas Geminus, *Moryssce and Damashin*, (London 1548).

18

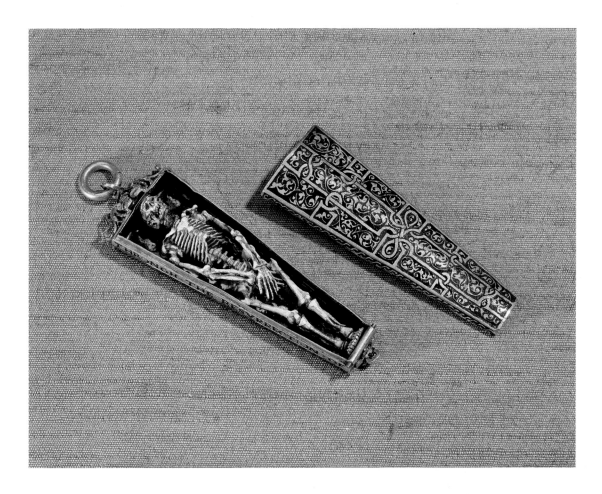

PLATE 13
Pendant, 'The Tor Abbey Jewel',
gold, decorated with enamel,
English, mid-16th century: h. 7.9
cms w. 1.9 cms (3⅛″ × ¾″).
3581–1856

in Devonshire where it was found. Jewels intended to remind one of the imminence of death were common throughout this period, and became even more so during the troubled times of the Civil War in England and the Thirty Years' War on the Continent (PLATE 14 *left*). Eventually their function was partly taken over by jewels worn in memory of the dead. PLATE 15 is an early example of such jewellery which made use of the hair of the deceased; in this instance the hair of one Eliz. Harman, who died aged 27 in 1698. The hair is placed under crystal with multifacetted edging, a dog-tooth setting characteristic of much mid- and late-17th century jewellery.

Some jewels were made in commemoration of a particular event or cause, especially in the 17th century. In England it was the Stuarts who were the most frequent subject, and PLATE 16 is an exceptionally verbose example. It is a miniature case engraved inside with an energetic, if rather poor, poem.

PLATE 16
Locket, copper-gilt. The front
engraved with the arms and motto
of Major William Carlos, the
reverse with Charles II and Carlos
hiding in the Boscobel oak.
English, second half of 17th century:
h. 6.2 cms w. 4.8 cms ($2\frac{7}{16}''$ x $1\frac{7}{8}''$).
898–1904

'Renewned Carlos!
Thow hast won the day
(Loyalty Lost) by helping Charles away,
From Kings-Blood-thirsty Rebels in a Night,
made black with Rage, of thieves, & Hells dispight
Live! King-Loved Sowle thy fame by Ever Spoke
By all whilst England Beares a Royall Oake.'

The 'Renewned Carlos' is Major William Carlos (died 1689) who
helped hide Charles II in the Boscobel oak after his defeat at the
battle of Worcester.

Throughout the whole period, but especially during the earlier
two centuries, gems were regarded as having prophylactic powers;
Jerome Cardan's *Gemmis et Coloribus* of 1587, for example, con-
sidered that the sapphire cured diseases of the skin, and that the
topaz cured madness and actually increased prudence and wisdom.
Both these stones are included in a pendant of around 1520–30

PLATE 17
Pendant, enamelled gold, set with
a topaz, almandine and sapphire,
German or English, 1540–30:
given by Dame Joan Evans,
h. 5.9 cms w. 2.8 cms
(2$\frac{5}{16}$″ × 1$\frac{1}{16}$″). M.242–1975

(PLATE 17) very similar to pendants shown in Holbein's portraits and designs; to reinforce the power of the stones it has the magical inscription on the back 'ANNA NISAPTA DEI. DETRAGRAMMATA. IHS. MARIÀ'. ANNA NISAPTA DEI was a common prophylactic for the falling sickness.

The design of the jewel is still rather simple, and it would have been worn around the neck, perhaps with a number of heavy gold chains. The effect would have been positively austere compared to the fashions of the second half of the century, when the Spanish liking for stiff jewel-encrusted dress dominated the courts of Europe. Francois Clouet's miniature of Caterina de Medici (1519–1589) (PLATE 18) shows her wearing this kind of costume with jewel-trellising on her bodice and one of the new matching *parures* of jewellery. On the head she has a head-dress or 'bordure', around the neck a short necklace called a 'carcan', and on the shoulders another

chain called the 'cotière'. Jewels also punctuate the ribbons of her
bodice and sleeves; indeed, it is clear from portraits that a great
deal of jewellery was sewn to clothing, and PLATE 19 shows some
very rare surviving examples of such secondary pieces.

As mentioned before, Queen Elizabeth carried the fashion for
spangling herself with jewels further than anyone else, and she was
also very fond of giving away images of herself, usually in the form
of jewels. She was not alone among the rulers of Europe in this
practice; it was the age when they were trying to extend their hold,
physical, political and spiritual, over the emerging nations of Europe,
and as a means of propaganda, they would have cameos and miniatures of themselves made, or would enclose medals of themselves
in precious settings. These were given away, perhaps at New Year,
and the receiver had an opportunity of displaying his loyalty by
wearing them. The Armada or Heneage jewel (PLATES 20–22) is one

19

21

20

22

of the most complex of these, with emblematic references of the kind that were favoured in European art and poetry of the time. According to the Heneage family, to whom it belonged until 1902, it was given by the Queen to Sir Thomas Heneage of Copt Hall, Essex, in recognition of his services as Treasurer at War during the time of the Armada (1587). It is in four parts: the front incorporates a gold bust of the Queen from the Personal or Garter badge of 1582 on a ground of translucent blue enamel, while the back shows PLATE 21 in basse-taille enamel an ark on the high seas. The motto SAEVAS TRANQUILLA PER VNDAS (Calm through the savage waves) surrounding it has three layers of meaning: the first refers to the success of the English fleet, and it also appears on the Naval Award medal of 1588; the second alludes to Elizabeth securely steering the Ship of State through political troubles; the third is a reference to her role as head of the Church of England, borrowing the age-old image of the Roman Catholic church as the ark. The back lifts to reveal a miniature by Nicholas Hilliard of the Queen (PLATE 22), her ruff covered with small jewels. The inner side of the back (PLATE 21) is decorated with a much more personal reference to her: a Tudor rose, symbol of her dynasty, is surrounded by a wreath of rose leaves, and, in humanist script, the quotation from a poem, 'Hei mihi quod tanto virtus perfusa decore non habet eternos inviolata dies' (Alas, that courage suffused with such great beauty does not last for ever inviolate).

Miniatures had become a very popular form of adornment, and maintained this popularity well into the 17th century. They were worn like pendants, sometimes around the neck, often pinned to the upper sleeve of the bodice, and sometimes hung from the girdle. As mentioned earlier, the fashion for intaglios and cameos had become widespread in the 16th century; classical examples, and those imitating the classical, were collected for treasuries and art-cabinets, and others were worn as jewels (PLATE 23). PLATE 24 shows one of the many cameo portraits of Queen Elizabeth, surrounded by enamelling characteristic of about 1600, with its small points of black on white and ogee shapes. Cameos of the Queen were part of at least one jeweller's stock in trade, for a handful of them were found, still unmounted, in the jeweller's hoard from around 1610 dug up from beneath a floor in Cheapside in 1912 (and now divided between the V & A and the Museum of London).

Pendants grew in popularity throughout the 16th century (FIGURE b), becoming very sculptural around the middle of the century, and then gradually more delicate, with much open work of C- and S-scrolls. More of them have survived than of any other sort of 16th century jewellery, except perhaps rings, and the forms they take are

PLATE 23
Ring, enamelled gold, set with a
cameo head of Medusa, German
or Flemish, c. 1575: diam. 2.5 cms
(1″). M.555–1910

PLATE 24
Pendant, the 'Barbor Jewel',
enamelled gold, set with an onyx
cameo of Queen Elizabeth, rubies
and diamonds, and hung with a
bunch of pearls, English,
c. 1590–1600: l. 6 cms w. 3.2
cms (2⅜″ × 1¼″). 889–1894

FIGURE b
Engraved design for a pendant
c. 1550 by Virgil Solis (1514–1562).

very varied. Religious pendants abound, but in addition there are examples with scenes from mythology, ships, camels, parrots and all manner of exotic animals.

Jewellery was often given to churches in gratitude for favours received and this practice greatly increased its chances of survival. PLATE 26 was one of the pieces which was given to the church of the Virgin of the Pillar at Saragossa, a pendant of a kind quite common in Spain well into the 17th century. This is a particularly fine one, with its scenes in embossed and enamelled gold. Many enclose a picture executed in *verre eglomisé*. The backs open to conceal a relic, and they were often worn on the ends of rosaries, attached by a knotted silken cord.

A most ingenious pendent jewel is a miniature wheel-lock pistol which is a combined whistle, earpick, toothpick and scraper (PLATE 27). The poor condition of the enamel is due to its having been in a fire in 1817, but one can still see the dense network of C-scrolls characteristic of the end of the century. Another functional jewel (PLATE 28) dating from the early years of the 17th century shows the delicacy and airiness of many pieces of the period; particularly characteristic are the beads of enamel in high relief. From the circular section, it is clear that it must have hung from a belt, rather than around the neck.

PLATE 25
Pendant, enamelled gold, set with rubies and hung with pearls, the figure depicting Orpheus or Apollo (the top element a 19th century replacement), German, *c.* 1600: h. 11 cms w. 5.7 cms (4⅝″ ✕ 2¼″). 2756–1855

PLATE 26
Reliquary pendant, rock crystal
and enamelled gold, set with
pearls, Spanish, *c.* 1580: h. 8.3 cms
w. 5.6 cms (3¼″ × 2³⁄₁₆″).
332–1870

PLATE 27
Pendant, the 'Pasfield Jewel',
enamelled gold, set with table-cut
emeralds, English, late 16th
century: l. 7.9 cms (3⅛″).
M.160–1922

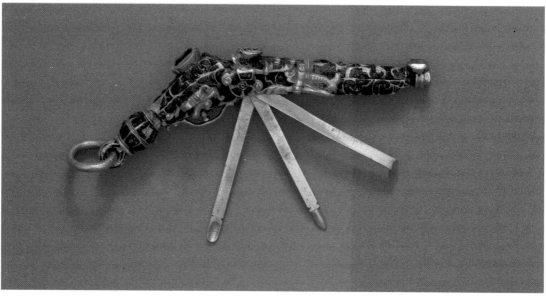

PLATE 29
Two aigrettes, pen and water-
colour drawing by Arnold Lulls,
c. 1610: h. 21.6 cms w. 15.5 cms
(8½″ × 6⅛″). D.6–19–1896.

If pendants have survived in abundance from the 16th century, many other sorts of jewels have almost totally disappeared; necklaces and chains set with large stones, for example, have nearly all been too valuable to escape being broken up. Consequently, the pictorial inventories which a few European princes had made of their jewellery are invaluable records of what is now missing. Duchess Anna of Bavaria commissioned Hans Mielich in 1556 to paint life-size miniatures of all her jewels, and Anne of Denmark, wife of James I of England, had hers painted by the Dutch jeweller, Arnold Lulls (PLATE 29). These vary in date from around 1550 to her own time, some indeed being very like the delicate creations found in the Cheapside hoard. The paintings are life-size, and most are of pendants or earrings, some clearly intended to be hung by ribbons from the ear. Four, however, are of magnificent assymmetrical gem-studded *aigrettes* with long tails for wearing in the bouffant hair fashionable at the time.

Although court jewels from all over Europe had achieved a considerable degree of uniformity in the 16th century, an occasional piece, particularly from Central Europe, perpetuates a local type. PLATES 30 and 31 illustrate this. The jewel is said to have belonged to Francis Rakoczy, Prince of Transylvania, and in the stones and the enamelling, which recall Prague court work of the same date, it is immeasurably finer than brooches belonging to less elevated Transylvanians. Nonetheless, it shows their form – the traditional brooch of the Transylvanians and Hungarians from around Brasov. Right up to the 20th century, such brooches were worn fastened to a velvet or embroidered silk and tied at the throat, or left to hang loose at the breast.

THE 17TH CENTURY

Jewellery design of the first thirty years of the 17th century tended to a greater abstraction than before. Plants became more stylised, colours less naturalistic. Typical of this development is the miniature case decorated with champlevé enamel in dramatic black and white (PLATE 32). This resembles a design by a Frenchman, Jean Toutin (FIGURE c), published in 1619; and such ornamentation could be adapted to other surfaces, as the large man's ring (PLATE 14 *right*) set with a vast smoked quartz. Similar ogival leaf shapes and beading appear on a watch of about the same date, with the pierced lid showing a rich swirling assymmetry (PLATE 33). By this date watches had become relatively common accessories; indeed, Henry VIII had given Catherine Howard three small 'clocks', one of which

PLATE 30
Brooch, gold, set with rubies and
diamonds and decorated with
enamel, Hungarian, *c.* 1600: diam.
6.4 cms (2½″). M.461–1936.

PLATE 31
Reverse of the above; the central
compartment contains a miniature.

was small enough to be enclosed in a pomander, and Elizabeth I had
what must have been one of the first wrist watches, an armlet of
gold 'all over fairely garnishedd with rubyes and diamonds having
in the closing thereof a clocke'. Watches did, however, tend to be
varied in form; some were cross-shaped, some fitted into small
silver skulls, and some were enclosed in large facetted crystals. But
while various forms continued in use in the 17th century, the custom-
ary oval or circular shape was developing.

The stylised leaf forms and swirling lines could also be adapted to
gem-studded pieces. A large breast-ornament (probably Dutch or
French), and an evolution from the pendant, shows how the funda-
mentally geometric cut of the stones has been softened by making
the deep gold setting leaf-shaped (PLATE 34). The whole piece is
constructed on three levels; a pierced backplate decorated with

36

black and white enamel, a convex jewelled front with touches of
enamelling, including the characteristic 'pea-in-a-pod' points of
white enamel, and the large jewels in their square settings which
screw through both the other layers and hold them together. This
kind of design and construction can be seen clearly in the designs of
another Frenchman, Pierre Symony, published in 1621 (FIGURE d).

These early decades of the 17th century saw a technical innovation
in enamelling with *émail en résille* on glass. This is a very delicate
process which seems to have been mastered by a very few French
workshops and one elsewhere, perhaps in Central Europe. It involves great skill in firing, for otherwise the glass background
shatters or melts, and even with scientifically controlled furnaces it
still presents many problems today. Most of the French pieces are

locket or watch cases (PLATE 35), but there is also a group of objects in Poland, mostly with narrow plaques attached, using the same technique, but in a very different style, with small jagged figurative scenes. Obviously the technique proved too demanding and it died out after only a decade; it was not to be revived until the end of the 19th century.

Around 1625–1630, fashion was revolutionised, and jewellery with it. The stiff patterned brocades and silks of the previous century were finally ousted by flowing plain materials in soft colours such as gold, pale blue, and grey. Hair was no longer piled up on the head, but worn in apparently natural ringlets loose on the shoulders. In looking at the portraits of the second half of the 17th century, one has the impression that sitters were aspiring to an informal simplicity, so little jewellery do they display (PLATE 36). Pearls were the only

PLATE 35
Pendant, enamelled gold, and hung with a pearl, French, *c.* 1610–20: given by Dame Joan Evans, h. 5.7 cms w. 3.2 cms (2¼″ × 1¼″). M.65– 1952

PLATE 36
Miniature painting of Catherine Murray, Countess of Dysart, by John Hoskins (*c.* 1595–1665), signed, and dated 1638: h. 22.2 cms w. 16.5 cms (8¾″ – 6½″). Ham House 274–1948

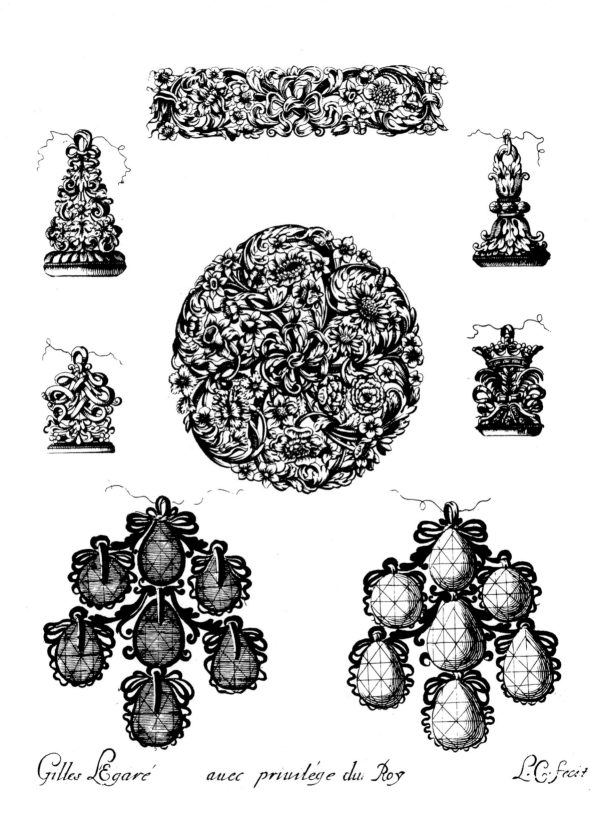

Gilles LEgaré   *auec priuilége du Roy*   *L. C. fecit*

essential adornment, their discreet gleam according well with the soft fabrics, and they were worn in the hair, around the neck, in the ears, and sometimes draped, baldric-wise, over one shoulder. There were not enough large pearls available to satisfy the demand, and, in the last quarter of the century, Parisian craftsmen ran a flourishing business in the production of fake pearls. Their technique was to remain unchanged for three hundred years: a blown globule of glass was lined on the inside with a nacreous substance made from the ground-up scales of the bleakfish (which can be found almost exclusively in the waters of the Seine) and then filled with wax to stabilise it.

Gem-cutting had also made progress with the *rose-cut*, which gradually emerged in the late part of the 16th century and became more and more important in jewellery designs. Rose-cut stones are clearly shown in those by Gilles Legaré, the important Parisian jeweller (FIGURE e). He also includes pieces intended to be decorated with luxuriant floral naturalism, a development in keeping with the botanical bias of all the decorative arts from the 1630s onwards, but closer examination, these designs all prove to be for watch cases, or for the painted decoration on the backs of jewellery. *Painted enamel*, which permitted a greatly increased naturalism, replaced basse-taille and champlevé almost completely in the second half of the 17th century.

Legaré's forms include the bow and the *girandole* which were to be fundamental to grand jewellery design right into the 19th century. A very characteristic example of the preoccupation with ribbons and bows is the necklace in PLATE 37, enamelled in pale blue with flecks of white and black – a very popular style in the middle of the 17th century. This necklace would have been enhanced by the real ribbon used to fasten it through the loops at the back.

In Spain the fashion was for a large breast-ornament and heavy earrings, and PLATE 38 shows one of these demi-parures. Some of the stones are set in the leaf-shaped settings evolved earlier in the century, and two metals, gold and silver, are used to complement the almandines and diamonds respectively. In this sumptuous jewel the bow shape is adapted to the heavy leafy baroque of the last quarter of the 17th century.

The pendant in PLATE 39 *left* is a suitable one with which to end this introduction to the jewellery of these three centuries, because it demonstrates the way in which 18th century jewels were to develop: the gemstones are closely set with a minimum of metal showing; their facetting is complex, with a foil behind them to reflect the maximum of light, and, apart from the cross, enamel has completely disappeared from the front of the jewel. Indeed, only

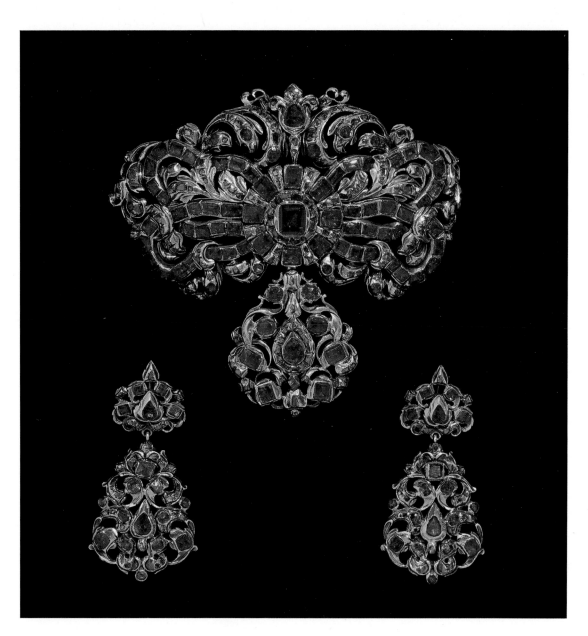

PLATE 37
Necklace, enamelled gold, set
with diamonds and hung with
pearls and cabochon sapphire,
probably French, c. 1670:
Bequeathed by Lady Alma-
Tadema, l. 36.5 cms d. 8.1 cms
($14\frac{3}{8}'' \times 3\frac{3}{16}''$). 95-1909

PLATE 38
Demi-parure, consisting of breast-
ornament and earrings, gold and
silver, set with diamonds and
almandines, French or Dutch,
c. 1670: given by Dame Joan
Evans, breast ornament w. 11.5
cms d. 10.5 cms ($4\frac{1}{2}'' \times 4\frac{1}{4}''$)
earrings l. 7.2 cms w. 3.6 cms
($2\frac{13}{16}'' \times 1\frac{7}{16}''$). M.98-1,b,c-1975

the general heaviness of design, and the scalloped settings to the central stone, reveal that this dates from the 17th century. Incidentally, it must have been a very expensive piece, for amethysts had only been discovered a few decades earlier in Catalonia, and throughout the 17th century they were prized above diamonds.

The jeweller, who had already during most of this century become distinct from the goldsmith, developed further specialisations, so that by the 1700s, the designing, gem-setting and enamelling would all have been done by different craftsmen. It is this division of labour as much as stylistic differences which distinguish later European jewellery from that of the 15th, 16th and 17th centuries.

Glossary

Aigrette A spray of gems worn in the hair or hat.

Arabesque or Moresque A scrolling pattern with stylised pointed foliage, of Islamic origin.

Bezel The broadening out, or ornamental top part, of a ring, as opposed to the shoulders or hoop.

Black letter The most commonly used scribe's hand throughout the fourteenth, fifteenth, and the early part of the sixteenth century; also the type-face used in the early days of printing. Supplanted by *Roman lettering*.

Cameo A gem, or sometimes a shell or other material, with a design or figure carved in relief. The material used usually consists of two or more layers of different colours so that the design is in contrast with the background.

Enamel a) *Bassetaille* The metal, usually gold or silver, is chased in very shallow relief and with depressions to provide the design, then completely covered with flux (ground glass plus the necessary pigments), often in more than one colour, and then fired and polished.

b) *Champlevé* Grooves are cut in the surface of the metal, then filled with the flux, and fired. The surface is then polished so that enamel and metal form one smooth surface.

c) *Painted* The flux, having been given a liquid medium, is painted onto a surface which is already enamelled, usually in one colour, and then fired. This allows the most realistic painterly effects to be achieved.

d) *Ronde-bosse* The flux is built up on the surface of the metal, which is usually modelled, much as gesso and paint are applied to the surfaces of wooden sculptures, and the object is then fired.

Girandole Jewels, especially earrings, with dependent drops.

Intaglio A figure or design cut into a gem-stone, or other material.

Memento Mori Literally, 'Be mindful of death': a work of art or jewel incorporating some symbol of death to remind the viewer of the transitoriness of life.

Morse The usually rather large clasp or fastening of a cope (the long cloak worn by the clergy on certain liturgical occasions).

Parure A matching set of jewellery. At different periods the sets comprised different elements, but in the 16th century they involved a head-dress, necklace, shoulder chain, and perhaps a pendant.

Roman lettering The letter form derived from Roman inscriptions.

Rose cut The cut for gems, especially diamonds, which involves a flat base to the stone, and a large number of triangular facets, usually 16 or 24, on the top.

Verre eglomisé Gold foil is applied to the back of a piece of glass and the design then cut and scratched into it, and sometimes enhanced with colours.

Bibliography

A. J. Collins, *Jewels and Plate of Queen Elizabeth I. The inventory of 1574* (London 1955). This is an invaluable work with which to supplement the study of existing jewels because it gives a clue to the types and quantities which are now missing, explains contemporary terminology and scales of value.

J. Evans, *English Posies and Posy Rings* (London 1931). This lists the inscriptions found on jewellery, giving the provenance of the jewel where it is known, and dates the various groups of inscriptions.

J. Evans, *Magical Jewels* (Oxford 1922). Dame Joan Evans's first book, a study of the magical powers attributed to jewels from classical antiquity to the 17th Century.

J. Evans, *A History of Jewellery 1100–1870* (London 1970 second Ed). The best general study of jewellery, to be supplemented by Steingräber (see below) who has a greater knowledge of the German scene.

F. Falk, *Edelsteinschliff und Fassungsform im Späten Mittelalter und im 16. Jahrhundert* (Ulm 1975). A detailed and very good study of actual jewels and depictions in painting of the manner in which jewels were cut and mounted from the 14th to the 16th centuries.

P. Muller, *Jewels in Spain 1500–1800* (New York 1972). The point of departure here is the volumes in the Barcelona town museum of jewellery designs submitted by aspirant masters to the goldsmiths' guild. The author also knows the archival sources well and illustrates numerous pieces and portraits.

C. Oman, *British Rings 800–1914* (London 1974).

C. Oman, *Catalogue of Rings* Victoria and Albert Museum (London 1930).

E. Steingräber, *Antique Jewellery: its history in Europe from 800 to 1900* (London 1957).